God and  in Music

CARL HALTER

Concordia Publishing House
Saint Louis

Concordia Publishing House   Saint Louis 18, Missouri
Concordia Publishing House Ltd., London, W. C. 1.
Copyright 1963 by Concordia Publishing House

Library of Congress Catalog Card No. 63-14990

10/19/77

MANUFACTURED IN THE UNITED STATES OF AMERICA

To My Wife, Miriam

PREFACE

The Christian cannot but constantly ask himself the question, "What difference does my faith make?" To answer this question, he must ask and answer another, "What difference does Christ make?"

These questions need to be applied to everything in the being and environment of a Christian, for if Christ and Christianity make no difference, they exist in vain. This book attempts an application of the questions to the art of music. If in the course of the book some thing or things are said which will impel the reader to listen and think for himself, the book will have fulfilled its intended function.

CARL HALTER

River Forest, Illinois
The Transfiguration of Our Lord, Feb. 11, 1962

CONTENTS

ACKNOWLEDGMENTS

In the summer of 1954 I was privileged to participate with Dr. Martin Marty and the now sainted Prof. Donald Meyer in a week-long symposium at Concordia Teachers College, River Forest, Ill., on the subject "Theology and Music." Some of the theological insights gained from them in that experience have found their way into this book, and I am happy to acknowledge my debt.

I should also like to thank my friend and colleague Prof. William Lehmann, Jr., for careful reading of the manuscript and for valuable suggestions.

1

Introduction

In these pages I shall be asking you to think about music. Thinking about music may strike some as being beside the point, or even impossible. We are accustomed to value and use music for a variety of reasons and in a number of situations. Even musical people, however, are inclined to overlook the contribution which music can make to man's understanding of himself and the world.

Most of us, surrounded as we are by music almost as inescapably as by air, have successfully pushed it into the background of our consciousness. This is often a matter of simple self-defense. Inferior music beats at our ears in a dreary whine in the home, in stores, and on the streets. Who would wish to listen attentively to this, much less think deeply about it?

The movies and television employ skillful and gifted composers. But very few people listen attentively to the music they write, nor is anyone expected to. Movie music is intended to provide an emotional setting in which a story can be effectively told; it is not intended to be noticed. It is above all not intended to capture the serious thought of the audience, for to do so would draw attention away from the story.

The conditions under which music is heard are more favorable in church and in the concert hall. In the first case the congregation is of a mind to listen because a large proportion of most public worship is in musical form. In the second case, music is the only thing going on, and in addition the audience has chosen to hear the particular music being performed and has paid for the privilege. But even in these two instances, music is usually valued for its emotional powers alone. Music, most people believe, is to be felt, or as it is more fashionable to say, experienced. The concertgoer or church member will usually say that he "enjoyed" the music or that a piece of music "moved" him.

While therefore all will agree that music has the power to generate and transmit emotion, few seem to recognize music's claim also on the mind. But the claim is there, and it is strong. The serious composer has a serious purpose, a purpose which is much more significant than the publicizing of his emotional states. His message includes his emotions, and they are important, as are those of the hearer, but his message includes also his view of himself, of other men, of the universe, and of God. Music is one of man's ways of exploring and subjecting to his purposes two great creations of God — sound and time — in such a way as to reveal the awesome wonders of both.

Because all this is so, I ask you to think as well as to feel, to keep a level head when you are excited about the glories of music, to "sing with the understanding also," as St. Paul has so simply summarized the matter.

I shall not ask you to think about all kinds of music because not all music demands or deserves serious thought. Entertainment music, for instance, requires only the ability to relax and to enjoy agreeable sounds. Such music serves a wholesome purpose, and we would all be much poorer without it. At its best it, too, gives us a glimpse into the heart of man and points to a legitimate relationship between man and his environment and, yes, even between man and God. But it is not, for all its virtues, music which demands very much or very deep thought.

There are bad composers, just as there are bad carpenters. There are greedy, mindless men who make bad music, just as there are greedy, mindless men who make bad chairs. Their products can support neither body nor spirit for long. From musicians of this sort comes the music which caters to the lowest levels of human consciousness and appeals to nothing higher. Such music should be considered only long enough to recognize it for what it is. Then it should be discarded. Such music perverts the great gifts of sound and time, debases man, and dishonors God.

In a day of feverish research into the construction and basic laws of the universe there is no need to demonstrate further that man constantly searches himself and his environment to find answers to the riddles with which life confronts him. Man uses also the art of music for this purpose. Our concern will be the music which seriously explores those mysteries of the world which are accessible to musical exploration — the mysteries of sound and time — and which earnestly seeks to communicate both the search and the findings. This is music which can and does capture the attention and concern of the whole human personality; this is music which can be thought about deeply; this is music which mankind finally finds to be significant and beautiful.

2

Music and Three People

M usic involves exploration and communication. The three people who participate in these processes are the composer, the performer, and the hearer. Each of them must take into account the other two when performing his own function.

A. THE COMPOSER

Composers write music for many reasons. They may wish to entertain or to provide a musical setting for other activities or to make money. The composer whose music is worth thinking about may have these purposes in mind, or others, but he is primarily concerned about making a discovery and showing his findings. Simply stated, his aim is by means of the manipulation of sound and time to discover some new facet of the significance of life.

The word "discovery" is a deliberate choice. No composer, it is safe to say, ever has the fully finished composition in his mind before he begins writing. Inevitably the very process of writing is a search for the correct, the appropriate, the revealing note or passage. This is why it takes so long to write a serious piece of music. The time is spent in exploring many blind alleys before the through avenue is discovered. The process is similar to the one which an author follows when he struggles to find the one word which will transmit his meaning precisely. The painter will paint and erase many times before he finds the correct amount of the appropriate shade of color.

All artists begin their work with an idea — an idea that is, in fact, their first discovery. For a composer the idea is a certain arrangement of tones and rhythms which excites him. It is not merely "catchy," but it has a significance which merits further exploration. Much is said about "inspiration." As this word is commonly understood it should be used to denote only this first step, the gift to the composer of the germinal idea which triggers him into exploration. The exploration plus the organization of the findings is the composition. However meaningful and beautiful, it is not the product of blind inspiration, received without effort and merely transcribed, but it is the product of hard and often frustrating work.

We have called the germinal idea a gift. It is that, but it, too, is not received without labor. The composer who spends his time thinking about stocks and bonds may get some fine ideas about investments, but he is not likely to receive an "inspiration" of melody. The composer thinks about music, imagines it, and is alert to recognize a good musical idea when it occurs to him.

The composer sets to work by writing out his idea. The idea may be a melody or theme, or it may be only a motif — a scrap of sound in time. Whatever its specific form or length or other unique features, however, it has a certain character which will largely determine the character of the composition.

Having written out his idea, the composer now sets out on his journey of discovery. He studies the idea, and the study produces other ideas in a long chain of relationships ever more distant from the original. As these thoughts grow out of one another, he organizes them into the composition. Some of them, perhaps most of them, he discards before they are written. Some of those he writes turn out to be faulty, inappropriate, or unclear. But now and again a passage has a certain rightness, or feeling of inevitability. He knows that this passage is a worthwhile discovery in itself and a sure foundation for other discoveries yet to be made.

We can see this process at work in its simplest form in the construction of a theme. The opening theme of Wolfgang Amadeus Mozart's *Symphony in G Minor* is based on a simple, brief idea:

Notice that the idea reaches upward, as if in question. Then follows an answer to the idea which comes down.

Now the idea and answer are repeated, but at a lower pitch level:

In the next part of the theme, only the first three notes are quotations from the original idea:

The preceding section ended on a note of expectation, which you can feel strongly if you play the theme up to this point. In answer to this expectation the original idea and its answer return:

Once again the idea and answer are repeated, but this time at a higher pitch rather than a lower:

The theme concludes with a passage leading to a contrasting theme.

The composer continues this process of exploring his materials and realizing yet other thoughts until the original idea is "worked out." This occurs when the composer feels instinctively that he has discovered all that he as one person can discover, and that he has organized his discoveries into intelligible form. Now he must trust his work to the performer. He is finished.

The composer is sorry when he is finished, and vaguely uneasy. Inevitably as he has written he has discovered himself, and he is displeased with some features of the discovery and uncertain and unsure about all of it. He is self-consciously or modestly hesitant to trust these discoveries to the performer and hearer. His inner self is to a greater or lesser degree wrapped up in this composition, and he is, like all other men, sensitive about his self. He knows that this composition in performance will be an act of revelation which will include his view of life, his emotions, his skills, and finally his worth as a musician and as a man. Hence his uneasiness.

Nevertheless, he will repeat the whole process whenever he gets another musical idea which excites him with the anticipation of still more discoveries. He will do this because for him the joy of music lies in the work of finding music in himself and in these two creatures of God — sound and time.

B. THE PERFORMER

We have said that the composer leaves his work at the point where he feels that he has discovered all that he, *as one person,* can find out about the subject of the composition. This is not to say that no other discoveries can be made. One of the great surprises and mysteries of all art is that there is always more to be found in a work of art than its maker is aware of or has consciously placed there.

This characteristic of music explains why performers and hearers have so much work to do, for the work and joy of discovery go on, not in the composer now, but in them. One of the signs of great music is that it generates many ideas in many people over long periods of time. Great music comes as an exciting discovery to generation after generation of performers and hearers. Poor music, in contrast, is stillborn and therefore unable to beget life in others.

As the performer first holds in his hands a piece of music which is new to him, it is likely to be a great puzzle. He needs to discover its secret code and its total meaning. The search for meaning is often made difficult, particularly in the new music of any age, by an unfamiliar language or dialect of language. "Why does the composer use these particular sounds, rhythms, combinations, structural principles? What is the form? What is his intent?" And finally, "Is this music to be taken seriously?" Remember, the performer is the first and most crucial judge of the merit of the composition.

Having as a result of his study decided that this music is worthy and having discovered wherein its worthiness consists, the performer sets about realizing his understanding of the piece. He practices and finds pleasure in practicing as long as he is trying ever better to reveal in his performance what he has found. Each performer will find something slightly different from every other performer and will give differing emphases to identical discoveries. These differences are of minor importance as long as they do not alter the essence of the composer's purpose and idea. Indeed, these differences serve to illustrate the fact that in any serious composition there are riches of meaning not all of which can be found and transmitted by any one person.

In order that these riches may be mined, the performer must manage a most difficult feat. He must remain true to the music as the composer wrote it and at the same time exercise a high degree of personal freedom. He is not merely the needle in a record's groove. He is the catalyst without whom no reaction can take place. The ideas must so take hold of him that they come through him to the hearer, not as though reported but as though believed. If this is done freely — conscientiously and yet without fear — audiences will catch the composer's vision as enlarged and enriched by the performer's. This sort of performance is the aim of all performers and the hope of all composers.

Now comes the performance. The nervousness of performers before concerts is universal. Some are so appalled at the prospect of performing, even after all their dedicated practice, that they seek to cancel the concert at the moment it is to begin. Some do. But think what is at stake! Not only their own livelihood and reputation though these are serious enough concerns) but also the continued existence of the precious idea and the resulting composition. The combined visions and discoveries of composer and performer are now to reach the stage of final revelation and judgment when the piece is played for the hearer.

And so the performer trembles as he wonders: "Will I be able to control myself and the instrument so that the music will be clear and all its parts in balance? Will I get the tempo, the intensity, the nuances just right so that the audience will understand?" And finally, "Will they find something in the music which will make them want to hear it again?" Remember, hearers finally decide whether or not a piece of music will live, either in its own time or perhaps later when other hearers and other times may prove more receptive.

C. THE HEARER

Now *you* must act. Notice the word "act." You must do more than sit and permit the music to be played. If in the opinion of composer and performer this music deserves a hearing and a judgment and you have agreed by your presence to try its case, you owe the music a fair trial. This will require work — work which is very similar to that of the other two collaborators.

Briefly stated, you also must make a discovery. This will not be easy, because, unlike the composer and performer, you have only one chance to consider the music. Once through and it is gone as far as you are concerned.

Because of this limitation, two things are required of you. In the first place, intense concentration. You will ordinarily not be able to study the music, so you must swallow it whole — all of it. Second, it is required of you that you suspend judgment until you have had time to digest what you have so hastily swallowed. This means that you will not make up your mind after the first few unfamiliar sounds but will continue to work on what you have heard long after the whole piece has been played. Remember that it took the composer and the performer months and even years to bring you their discoveries. You cannot make yours in an infinitesimal fraction of that time.

D. THE COMMON OBLIGATION

All three participants in the musical activity have one obligation in common — the obligation of discovery. The objects of discovery we shall discuss later, but it must be clear now that it is the *act of discovery* which must occupy the attention of all three.

If the composer wishes to be taken seriously, he has the obligation to bring to his performer and his hearers some new light, some new insight, some new profundity of understanding. If he merely puts together some pretty sounds, what is that? His value to his partners lies in enlarging their view. His partners will not thank him if he trades in the obvious. His partners will be less than grateful also if, having a vision, he fails to make it clear. They will not thank him if he trades in obscurity, in private visions kept private.

The performer is similarly bound to the composer by the common obligation to discover. He is responsible to the composer to transmit his vision faithfully, with integrity. He must not seek sensuous effects which would obscure the reality beneath the sounds. He must not impose himself on the music, for what is he? He is a "voice crying in the wilderness" to sing a song which is not his own but which he has received from another. To transmit faithfully, he can and must make it his own, but he must not change the vision into something which reveals only his own little self.

The performer is at the same time the only means by which the hearer can make his discovery, and so the performer has a similar obligation also to him. Fortunately the hearer asks the same thing as does the composer. The hearer also asks to hear the truth of the music presented simply, clearly, and with conviction.

Finally, the hearer has the obligation of discovery no less than the composer and performer. It is for his discovery that they have made theirs at such great cost. Furthermore, the contribution which music will make to an individual's life will vary directly with the amount of effort which he puts into the work of discovery. This is not what is usually understood by the word "appreciation." One may esteem a composer's or performer's labor or talent or technical mastery without having discovered anything of value to one's life. All this is nothing unless there is also an understanding of and participation in his vision — a realization of the composer's idea in one's own mind and spirit.

There are three people, only one task. There is much serious music but only one purpose for all of it. This is to discover and reveal what is already inherent in the created world and what is within the grasp of our fumbling hands.

3

Music and Three Powers

Now we turn to three mysterious powers. We have already considered mysteries in speaking of the composer, the performer, and the hearer. How, for instance, is it possible to *think* in tones and in time periods, without words and what are usually thought of as concrete ideas? How is it possible for anyone to think in terms so immaterial, so indefinite in meaning, and which leave so little trace? We know that it is possible because it happens, but *how* it is possible remains a mystery.

At this point we wish to attempt a deeper look into the phenomenon of music by examining three of its basic powers: (a) the power to be, (b) the power to grasp, and (c) the power to speak.

A. THE POWER TO BE

The greatest of all wonders in the world of art is the wonder that such a thing as music can be. This is no less a wonder and mystery because we take it for granted. We take all the basic wonders of life for granted, beginning with the mystery of life itself.

Think for a moment what a wonderful power it is in the mind of man that he can draw a few lines on paper and that in obedience to these lines materials will be gathered from all their scattered places of creation and assembled to build the Parthenon or your own room. What a mastery of life is involved when a novelist selects and organizes the stuff of living into a form which imparts meaning to life! What a power operates when a painter conjures from lines and colors smeared on a flat surface of cloth his vision of the world.

No less a mystery is presented to us in a piece of music. Someone has taken the whole range of audible sound and all the time available to man, and has so selected, manipulated, and organized these that an intelligible entity has been created. It sounds impossible, and it would be except for two facts: all the elements of nature have been so created that they permit of exploration, manipulation, and ordering, and man has been so created that he has the power to do these acts.

But the mystery remains and it is like the mystery of life. What is it that makes one composition dead and another alive? What makes one piece so important to us that we will not let it go but demand to hear it again and again, and another piece so inconsequential that we cannot remember it even after repeated hearings, except perhaps with annoyance?

We shall have something to say to these questions as we go along, but our answers will still leave many questions behind. It is best to recognize early that here is a mystery, the mystery of being. When you listen to a piece of music, begin your response with the recognition that you are witness to a miracle.

B. THE POWER TO GRASP

Music has not only the power to exist as a thing in itself, but it has also the power to grasp living meanings which lie both within and outside its essence. Music is meaningful, having a significance of its own, and is also and at the same time a tool with which to grasp and manipulate meanings which reside outside itself in the universe, in God, and in man. It is like water, which by itself can be an ocean or rain and which in combination with other things can become a tree or a potato or the bulk of the body of a man.

The Intrinsic Grasp

A well-written piece of music has intrinsic meaning. This meaning inheres in it in that it exists, much as a tree or a sunset have meanings for us which do not depend on anything outside themselves. The significance of music *as music* cannot be translated into an essay on love, for instance, or on any other concrete or philosophical subject. Music means something in itself and on its own terms.

The intrinsic meaning of music arises out of its use of two natural phenomena, sound and time. When we speak of music's intrinsic meaning, we must eliminate from our thoughts all extraneous matters such as a "program," story, or other literary references which might tend to impose extramusical meanings on the music. The purposeful organization of sound and time imparts to music a meaning which is all its own.

The basic way in which the composer achieves meaning in music is through order, or form, and through purposeful deviations therefrom. There is a heresy which implies that because freedom is good, law and restraint are bad. This is a false conclusion in all of life, including the arts. Through the imposition of restraint, our acts can cease to be random, purposeless, and even destructive and can instead become reasoned, purposeful, and constructive.

So it is in music. To bang one's hand on the piano as one walks past will result in sound but not in music. It is only as the composer selects certain sounds, limits their time, and places them in a certain order and relationship to one another that music is created. This act involves the composer's total being — his intelligence, his emotions, his sensitivity, his training and experiences, his likes and dislikes, and whatever else in him could affect his choices among myriads of possibilities before him. In a very immediate sense the music will *mean what he is.*

The Manipulation of Sound

In order to illustrate the fact that the purposeful selection and ordering of sounds in sequence and in time imparts meaning to music, let us consider a composer's use of the major scale of Western music. This scale is in itself already a purposeful arrangement of sounds; it serves to lead a hearer from a tone to its octave by means of eight predetermined steps. It is also so thoroughly known to all Western peoples that it serves the composer as a fund of basic musical understandings which he can manipulate to his purpose.

Since the major scale is so thoroughly known, it is also the *expected* sequence of notes in any scale passage.

28

We take for granted that when we have heard C D E F, we shall next hear G A B C. If the composer uses the scale in this form he has satisfied the hearer's expectation. The meaning of such a simple scale passage is, then, *affirmation*.

But let us say that the composer, instead of going on with G A B C, goes back down, F E D C, or skips, E C A. In these cases he has set up the expectation and then denied it. He may be said to have rejected the inevitability of the expected fulfillment. The meaning of such a simple device is *rejection*.

Or let us look at another example, that of chord progressions in the Western tonal system. Through a long process of development, Western music has established a hierarchy among the triads (chords) which are formed with the steps of the scale as their roots. One of the most powerful laws of the relationship of triads is that the V chord (G B D in the key of C) finds its natural resolution in the I chord (C E G in the key of C). We have come to expect that whenever the V chord is heard, the I chord will follow immediately. The composer may and often does affirm the normality of this expectation.

V   I

But often he does not and goes instead from the V to the VI (A C E), for example, creating what is called a "deceptive cadence," or he may retrogress, going from the V to the II (D F A). In these latter cases, he has rejected the expectations of the hearer — deceived him or startled him into a fresh awareness.

V   VI   V   II

These are pictures in miniature of all composition and primitive examples of how music develops intrinsic meaning through the manipulation of sound. It should be said that here affirmation is not to be equated with good and rejection with evil. Nor do affirmation and rejection here mean positive and negative or true and false in any antagonistic sense. Rather, affirmation is to be understood as *statement* and rejection as *contrast*. The composer needs and uses both devices in order to make his meaning clear.

Particular expectations are set up also in each individual composition. The composer does this when he announces his theme or basic material. This is now "normal" for the piece of music, both for the composer and for the hearer. But the composer alters his material and turns it this way and that, as though to say, "Let's see how it would sound if we changed a note here, or if we wrote it upside down, or if we wrote it in different keys." In his experimentation he alternately affirms, denies, alters, expands, and contracts his original statement until at the end of the piece he states a final triumphant reaffirmation.

In Chapter 2 we watched Mozart as he "discovered" the theme of the first movement of his *Symphony in G Minor* (p. 17). Now let us observe how Mozart ex-

Violin

plored his material, altering it in a number of ways to show all its facets. At the beginning of the development section we find the first part of the theme altered by placing it in a number of different keys. Notice also that only a part and not the whole theme is examined repeatedly.

There is much more of this sort of development than we have reproduced here. In addition, Mozart throws the theme from one instrument to another so that we may hear the theme in a number of different tone colors. Later Mozart takes only the first three notes of his theme for still further examination. Notice that he inverts the figure and uses it antiphonally and in combination with itself.

After this intensive exploration the theme is restated in its original form and the movement is concluded.

One kind of intrinsic musical meaning is what we have been calling affirmation and rejection. But this is only one kind. The list could be extended considerably without once borrowing from experiences outside the music itself. Other pairs of concepts inherent in music are unity and diversity, tension and release, growth and decline, rise and fall.

You will note from this brief list that conflict is at the heart of musical meaning. Music always moves, and since it moves, it must always move away from something and toward something else. This very movement implies conflict among choices and always has meaning, since it is selective, purposeful, intellectually calculated and controlled.

In addition to the processes we have discussed, there are many other devices by which musicians manipulate sound. Among these are —

a) Harmony, the support of a melody with chords, as in a hymn tune;

b) Counterpoint, the use of two or more melodies simultaneously, as in a fugue;

c) Dynamics, the use of varying degrees of loudness to provide emphasis and contrast;

d) Tone color, as produced by instruments and voices, singly and in combination, which differ from one another in the nature of their tone, e. g., flute and trumpet; and

33

e) Texture, which in music is said to be thick or thin according to the number of voices sounding simultaneously.

The Manipulation of Time

The intrinsic meaning of music is no less a product of the manipulation of time. The factor of time plays a dual role. In the first place, it exists as a separate entity in the music and can hold the hearers' interest for itself. Rhythmic drive or rhythmic complexity is sometimes the chief feature of a composition, as it is in Maurice Ravel's "Bolero," for example. African music has developed the separate manipulation of time to a high degree of sophistication — much higher than we have in the Western world.

In occidental music the manipulation of time commonly serves mainly as an additional device for the manipulation of the sounds. Time participates along with harmony, counterpoint, and the rest in the development of meaning in music. Perhaps the simplest way to illustrate the crucial role played by time is to show how a well-known melody is changed in character when the temporal relationships of its notes are disturbed. Here is the stately melody of the fine English hymn tune "St. Anne," by William Croft.

Our   God, our Help in   a - ges past

Now see how the character of this dignified melody is altered by setting the same notes in three-four time.

A vigorous melody has become a stodgy, bumbling waltz.

A different rhythmic change makes the tune a more sprightly but still awkward waltz.

The notes which William Croft used become the tune "St. Anne" only when they are heard in the time relationships of the first example.

The chief devices for the manipulation of time include —

a) Rhythm, the pulses (recurring accents) of the music grouped into patterns, normally multiples of two or three;

b) Tempo, the speed at which the music moves;

c) Rhythmic patterns, combination of note values

within the established rhythm into interesting "time formulas," a device on which the excitement of much contrapuntal music is dependent; and

d) Rubato, hastening or delaying the appearance of a note.

We began this section on intrinsic meaning by noting that a composer imparts meaning to his composition through form. Form is the total of all the forces, elements, and devices of which we have spoken, put into balance and order, made rational and intelligible. It is that intelligent direction of sound in time which sets up expectations, retards their fulfillment, and then fulfills them.

A Deeper Grasp

So far we have spoken only of the musical meanings which are limited to the notes themselves. Now, still without borrowing from any extramusical concepts, we wish to take note of allied meanings which music grasps.

You will have noticed that the intrinsic meanings are so universal that they are true not only of music. We find affirmation and rejection, unity and diversity, growth and decline in all of life. When the composer therefore places sounds in such form that they speak of these matters, he grasps them not only for his little piece but, as in a mirror, for all of life. The composer says implicitly: "Here is how the experiences of life sound. I cannot explain them to you, but I can make them sound. After you have heard how they sound, you will understand them better and have for all of life a sympathy which you did not have before and which you cannot get in any other way."

Listen carefully to a recording of Beethoven's *Fifth* or *Ninth Symphony* or to any of Bach's gigantic organ fugues, and within the music you will hear struggles which can only be described as titanic. The composer has set in motion gigantic forces of sound and time which clash and contend to a climax of fury. On listening to such music it becomes obvious to us that the composer did not manipulate these massive forces merely to show that they exist and that he has the skill and strength to control them. An attentive and expectant listener inevitably is convinced that the composer has grasped forces and meanings which go far beyond the music and which relate to all of life. Indeed, such music convinces us that the grasp of music extends, however feebly, to the divine and the eternal. Such music gives us an apprehension of ultimate reality, ultimate values, and ultimate destiny.

Music probably reaches farthest into these ultimate realms and closest to the experience of the divine not in its moments of fury and contention but in its quiet, contemplative, searching moods. It is axiomatic that to know a composer one must know the slow movements of his works. Listen to the long, seemingly wandering, bittersweet, slow movements of the Brandenburg concertos of Johann Sebastian Bach, for instance, or to the slow movements of the symphonies of Johannes Brahms, Ludwig van Beethoven, or Mozart. You will hear a wide variety of mood, but under all the undulating surfaces can be felt an attitude of pondering and a discourse with others who likewise ponder.

The element of discourse is an extremely important

37

factor in much great music. In music of the contemplative type the composer seems to try to involve the listener very intimately in his search for meaning. An excellent example of such intense musical conversation is found in the second movement of Bach's *Brandenburg Concerto No. 6,* where two violas participate in a quiet, brooding dialog of great beauty.

As the composition continues, the two voices singly, alternately, and together explore the subject intensively.

It seems significant that the piece does not end in the key (E Flat Major) in which it begins, but rather on the chord D F Sharp A, which in its use here is the dominant (V) chord of the key of G Minor. This equivocal conclusion of the piece gives one an unsatisfied, unfulfilled feeling. Bach seems to say that the search has not been concluded in this music. He and we together must pick up the search at another time.

Certainly in music such as this the composer is searching out the sounds he has before him, but he is doing much more than that. He is searching out the enigmas of life; he is showing us that things in life are like things in music; he is asking us to learn the music so that we may know and understand more of life; he is pointing to something beyond the music and even beyond the life which we now experience to a life beyond sound, beyond time — another life which he knows is there because he feels the need for it and which he knows is waiting for him because he finds no ultimate affirmation or fulfillment in this one, not even in his music as he writes it.

Such music awakens longings it cannot satisfy. The longing to hear pretty sounds can be satisfied easily and quickly reaches the point of satiety. Interest in a composer's technical mastery is of longer duration, but does not take us beyond the mechanics of the music. The search for ultimate answers to the ultimate questions is, however, a desperate lifelong pursuit for all men. Music is such a great gift to mankind, not because it gives the ultimate answers before their time but because it impels man to the search and gives him another arena for it. The wordless quest is appropriate to the unknowable.

You will note that there is a mixture of the psychological, emotional, philosophical, and intellectual in the intrinsic meanings grasped by music. There is no absolute parallel with meanings found in any other field of human action or thought. Intrinsic musical meaning is a thing unique to music. This is one reason why man is, to imitate a famous remark, incurably musical. There are things he can do and say in music which he cannot do or say in any other form of expression.

All these things music does without once asking the aid of any concept outside itself — simply by being music, without a word spoken, without a title, without a picture, without even the slightest suggestion that one should hear this or that. And because this is so, the intrinsic meaning of music is the most valuable to the human spirit. For this avenue to the meaning of life can be traveled only here.

The Extrinsic Grasp

When music is acclaimed as a universal language, it is the intrinsic meaning of music which is meant. You will note that the intrinsic meanings are very broad, general, even vague and elusive. Such lack of specific identification is what makes the universality of music possible. The meanings are so general that they fit all mankind and are experienced by all mankind.

Western music certainly has these meanings, but a Western listener can hear them in the most strange oriental or "primitive" music as well. To test this point, listen to African music long and intently enough to overcome the initial strangeness. You will hear the intrinsic meanings. It makes no difference that the tonality is not our own or that the instruments are strange to us or that the African has chosen to develop rhythm rather than harmony. The movement, conflict, and resolutions are still there. There is form, order, control. There is even in the tenderer moments of African song the same yearning toward the ineffable and unattainable.

There are, however, other meanings which music grasps and which are not universal in character. These are the "extrinsic" meanings. They are dependent on something which lies outside the music in the general culture of which the music is a part. The process involved is the association of ideas. Experiences, moods, and even concrete objects and ideas are identified rather specifically, and music is deliberately written to represent and convey these concepts. Since these meanings depend for their apprehension and communication on knowledge of a culture, it is unlikely that they are ever universal in character. Much of the associative or extrinsic meaning of Chinese music, for example, escapes the Western listener because the music arises out of and makes reference to a specific culture of which we have inadequate knowledge and experience.

To communicate these extrinsic meanings, the composer must tell the hearer by means of a title, "program," or other device what he intends. For example, Felix Mendelssohn-Bartholdy, in one of his *Songs Without Words,* wrote a piano piece which used as its basic idea the imitation of the sound of a spinning wheel. To ensure that the hearer would understand, he gave the piece the title "Spinning Song." Robert Schumann once wrote a series of piano pieces called *Phantasiestücke* ("Fantasy Pieces"). In this series are pieces titled "Whims," "Why?" and "In the Night." One of the clearest examples of the attachment of extramusical ideas to musical figures is found in the delightful orchestral fairy tale, *Peter and the Wolf* by Serge Prokofieff. A narrator participates in the performance and explicitly specifies the characters associated by the composer with each musical motif. Among these three examples we find imitation of non-musical sound, designations of states of mind or emotions, and identification of character.

Another example of the associative power of music

is Modest Moussorgsky's *Pictures at an Exhibition,* in which the composer attempted to translate into sound the meanings he found in paintings hung in a gallery. One hears the composer enter the room, contemplate each picture, and then walk to the next. It is quite successful *if* you know the pictures. In fact, all extrinsic meanings depend on knowing something outside the music. A person who has not been told the title will not be able to tell that the piece "Whims" was intended by Schumann to be an expression of whimsicality. The person who has never heard a spinning wheel in action will miss much of the feeling Mendelssohn meant to convey. If *Peter and the Wolf* were played without the narration, no listener would be able to reconstruct the story. Those who have not seen the pictures Moussorgsky had before him (and this includes most of us) will never fully grasp the music's meaning.

For churchgoing people, one of the common experiences of the power of association is to hear organ music based on a hymn. The tune and text have become so closely identified that the worshiper hears the words in his mind as the organ plays the tune. Conversely, the words call forth the tune. Anyone wishing to test the power of this particular association should try to change the tune of a hymn whose melody has become well known and well loved.

The associative power of music goes far beyond the simple and somewhat obvious uses so far referred to. Perhaps no composer ever made more extensive use of this power of music than Richard Wagner in his operas. For each character and for each dominant theme Wagner constructed a leitmotiv, a melodic phrase or passage associated with the particular person or idea throughout the opera. In the well-known love-death section of *Tristan und Isolde,* for example, the themes for Tristan, Isolde, love, and death are intertwined in the orchestra in a marvelous way to represent the drama at the climactic moment. If the listener knows the motifs and for whom or what they stand, he is able to hear in the music what he sees on the stage. The music and the action are specifically associated, and they illuminate each other.

Composers of the baroque period (1600—1750) used the extrinsic grasp of music as one of their chief means of developing meaning in their works. An entire philosophy of composition, called *Die Affektenlehre* ("the doctrine of the affections") was developed, in which each composer created his own musical motifs to denote the subjects being treated in his music. Usually these motifs were associated with an individual word in the text or to a thought which underlay the entire text or a specific portion. Examples of this procedure are to be found throughout Bach's music for the church. One typical example is found in his cantata *God's Time Is the Best.* In the chorus "It is the Old Decree, Man, Thou Art Mortal," Bach employs not only a counterpoint of notes but a counterpoint of ideas represented by the notes. The three lower voices sing the title words of the chorus, employing as the distinctive feature of their theme the diminished-seventh interval, which in Bach's table of equivalents represents death, fallenness, despair, and the darker emotions generally:

44

It is the old de - cree

The soprano voice is reserved for the expression of faith and hope and therefore never sings the theme shared by the other three voices. The words of the soprano part are "Yea, come, Lord Jesus, come," and the music is based on motifs which Bach consistently used for the idea of beseeching or coaxing:

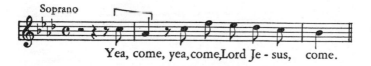

Yea, come, yea, come, Lord Je - sus, come.

Yea, come, Lord— Je - sus,— come.

These two elements enter into an extended contest. First the three lower voices seem to be marching inexorably toward the victory of the grave over life, but again and again the soprano's message of trust and hope enters, always a little stronger than before. Finally, at the end of the chorus, the three lower voices are "overcome" by the soprano prayer. They reach a climax of intensity and power in their struggle for supremacy, and then, at the height of their effort when victory seems assured, they just stop singing while the soprano part continues serene and sublime to the conclusion of its triumphant prayer.

Significantly, the soprano voice is singing the name "Jesus" when the three lower voices with their message of mortality are overcome.

While all of this is going on, the chorale *Ich hab'*

S.

— — sus, Lord Je-sus!

mein' Sach' Gott heimgestellt ("I Cast My Care upon My God") appears in the orchestra.

Flute

(I cast my care up - on my God.)

To measure such music by its auditory appeal alone (although this is great indeed) is absurd. Obviously Bach here presents a life-and-death drama which is universal in its meaning for human life. He presents also an answer to the problem he describes. For Bach, as for all Christians, the answer to the power of death is the power of the Lord Jesus Christ. And Bach says it, dramatizes it, and makes us feel it *in music.*

The almost incredible richness and complexity of meaning which Bach imparts to his music by this means is one of the great intellectual delights of all music. One who knows the symbolism which Bach employs will find endless reward in the study of his music, not only on the level of beautiful sound but on eminent intellectual, philosophical, and spiritual levels as well. There can be no doubt that Bach grapples with the great questions of life, death, and destiny. There can be no question that he does so in music. Our own contemplation of the ultimate concerns is illuminated and enriched by knowing and considering his.

You will note that the associations we have so far pointed out have been made by the composer's deliberate choice. So that these associations may communicate accurately, it is necessary that the composer inform the hearer in some way. There is, however, another whole area of associative or extrinsic meaning about which the composer needs to say nothing, because the hearer within a culture already knows the associations. For example, if a Western composer wishes to impart a religious feeling to his music, he need only use Gregorian chant or the modality in which the chant is written. This modality differs from the tonality in which Western music has been written since about 1600 and is instantly recognizable as a "religious" style. The unique tonality and cadence of American Negro music, the particular movement and style of an 18th-century minuet, or the lilt of a 19th-century waltz — each instantly connotes in our minds a whole constellation of associations.

So powerful are these rather general extrinsic associations that they sometimes constitute a hazard for the composer. He may be trying to write about one thing and inadvertently trigger quite different thoughts in the hearer through use of an idiom or reference which symbolizes a contrary or inconsistent set of associations. There are, for instances, many pieces which employ the following very common phrase in approximately the same rhythm:

One of these which comes to mind at the moment is Bach's lovely organ prelude on "A Child Is Born in Bethlehem," in which these are the last four notes. Unfortunately they happen also to be the first four notes of the well-known, lighthearted lament, "How Dry I Am." This is very distressing!

There is hazard also in the fact that the significance of generalized idioms often changes. Today the minor mode is likely to be associated in the popular mind with sadness. It was not always so. Mozart's *Symphony in G Minor* is anything but sad. Much of it is sprightly, if not downright gay.

There is a particularly difficult problem for composers who have the need to say something in music for which no present associations exist or for which no existing associations are adequate in power. It becomes their task to create new or altered associations and consistently to employ them in their work so that eventually the hearer will comprehend. In a sense the problem is to construct a new foreign language. Even if their chosen language is not a new one, it may be so personal a form of expression, so intense, or so lofty, that it is not immediately or widely understood.

It is partly for this reason that some great composers do not find their best and most appreciative audiences until long after death. This certainly was true of Bach, whose own sons valued their father's compositions less than they should have and many of whose works lay forgotten for

80 years until Mendelssohn began the Bach revival with his presentation of the *St. Matthew Passion* in 1829. But I believe that even Mozart, who was more popular than Bach in his own time, has come to mean more to us today than he meant to his contemporaries. Béla Bartók died in 1945, and yet it has been only recently that his works, particularly his string quartets, have begun to attract the interest they deserve. Many more years will undoubtedly pass before his full worth is properly appraised.

This is not to say that all attempts at new musical language and idiom are equally valid and will prove equally capable of capturing vital meanings. Impressionism, the sensuous and lovely music which saw the Romantic period into its grave at the turn of the 19th and 20th centuries, proved too fragile and wispy a style to bear the burden of large thoughts. We still do not know the fate of atonalism, although recent developments seem to indicate that its contribution may be largely one of clearing away the debris of the wrecked harmonic system to make way for yet another kind of speech.

In all this it must be remembered that the musician acts not only for himself but also as a responsible agent of his society. The culture within which he moves also acts on him even as he acts on it. The extrinsic meanings which his music grasps are likely to be in great part those which concern his fellowmen as well as himself.

Perhaps we can now agree that music has the power to grasp extrinsic meanings through the process of association and that much music depends for much of its significance on this grasp. Let us also recognize, however, that most people never learn enough about the external frame of the music they hear to enjoy this rich area of meaning. What is left, if anything?

For one thing, the most important meanings, the intrinsic meanings, are present in all kinds of music — music which has explicit extramusical connotations as well as so-called abstract, or pure, music. For another, even music which has heavy literary references, such as the tone poems of Richard Strauss, can be listened to with great enjoyment and profit entirely without knowledge of the "program." Wagner's great opera music is heard less and less in full dramatic performance and more and more in concert simply because it is fine music as it stands. In well-written programmatic music the program serves the composer as an impetus for the creation of themes and as a suggested structure. The themes and structure thereupon have lives of their own and are capable of capturing meanings totally unrelated to the original program.

This makes it possible for the hearer to construct his own connotations. When Schumann wrote "Whims," he undoubtedly thought of his own whims or of those of some close friend. It will make no difference to Schumann or his friend or anyone else if we hear in the piece our own whims or those of someone else whom we know well. In fact, it will make no difference to anyone if we fail to hear any whims at all and hear instead stampeding buffalo on an open prairie at dusk or even only some interesting and momentarily captivating music. Perhaps you, like most of us, can never remember the names of the individual dances in Petr Tchaikovsky's *Nutcracker Suite*. It is, however, a matter of sublime indifference whether we are listening at the moment to the "Dance of the Sugar-Plum Fairy" or the "Dance of the Flutes."

All is therefore by no means lost if the hearer is ignorant of the full intent of the composer and the full setting and function of the piece he hears. But enough is lost to impel us to know and learn more than we ordinarily do about the music we hear. The more we know, the more discoveries we will make in the music itself, the deeper the meanings we will find, and the more our whole selves, including our minds, will be captured and nourished by these otherwise seemingly arbitrary sounds.

C. THE POWER TO SPEAK

We have been considering the power of music to grasp meanings, but it has been impossible to speak only of the grasp of music without also making reference to the power of music to communicate what it has grasped. The only purpose of the grasp is that the music may speak.

All art is created so that the maker may reveal to his fellowmen something of importance that he has found. No artist is so lonely as the one whose works fail to speak; and no art is so sterile. It is not enough for a piece of art simply to be, wonderful as this is. It is not enough for a piece of art to have grasped meanings, necessary as this is. The meanings must be transmitted to others before they can have the life sought for them by the artist.

The life sought by the artist for his work is not simply that of understanding and admiration; he is intensely concerned that the vision of life which his work has grasped may move those to whom it is addressed and may change them in a significant way. This is what we mean by the "power to speak," not only that the message be understood but that it be believed and elicit a response in emotion and action. The artist wants his work to be used; he seeks involvement in the life outside his art.

Because of this intense desire not only to communicate understanding but to beget new attitudes and to incite action, many new movements in the arts have the aspect of protest. The "angry young men" of recent English fiction produce a literature of social protest. *Les Fauves* ("the wild beasts") of France in the early years of this century were painters who earned their appellation by the revolutionary nature of their paintings. Richard Wagner was a political and social rebel who wrote political pamphlets as well as revolutionary opera.

The picture of the artist as an emasculated wraith sulking in an ivory tower or cowering behind a locked basement door is indeed a caricature. No one cares more about all of life and mankind than the true artist. It is finally for this reason that he makes his art and hopes so desperately that it will speak to his fellows for their good.

It is undoubtedly much easier to see this power of art as it shows itself in the more concrete and representational arts of sculpture, painting, architecture, and literature than it is to see it in music. Particularly in literature the artist is able to argue and document his case quite explicitly, as is done, for example, by Jean-Paul Sartre and other existentialist writers. Anyone acquainted with the paintings of Goya's later life can see his bitter protest against the inhumanity of his time in Spain (1746—1828). If one walks through a home designed by the late Frank Lloyd Wright, one recognizes that the occupants would have to adjust not only their furniture but their lives as well. His architecture, like all worthy architecture, is an expression of his beliefs regarding how people should live.

Since music cannot use concrete symbols, it is difficult to see how music speaks to the same effect as the other arts. But speak it does and in terms which are quite recognizable. Why else would the leaders of Soviet Russia be concerned with Dimitri Shostakovich as well as Boris Pasternak? What made a special *motu proprio* of Pope Pius X necessary in 1903? In the first case the Russian commissars for art have recognized that music, too, can undermine their attempts at complete control of all life. They recognize that the smell of freedom can be detected also in music. In the second case, Pope Pius found it necessary, quite properly, to remind the church of the function of music in the church, so that a tendency toward secularization might not destroy its usefulness for the spiritual life of the faithful. Whatever the merits of either case, however, it is clear that music was speaking and speaking in the way and to the effect that we are here considering.

It must be recognized, however, that music's chief effort at speech is directed toward the inner life of the individual man. The polemicist and social or governmental revolutionary will rarely turn to music to advance his cause. He will turn to literature and painting much more readily, because in these he can be more explicit. In instances in which music gives rise to mass action, as in the case of patriotic songs and fervent evangelistic hymns, it is usually the combination of words and music which is effective. The musician is much more likely to be concerned with what a man is than with what men do. His art seeks to establish in his fellowman the understandings, attitudes, and emotions which he feels are necessary for man's personal life and for man's relationships with the universe, with other men, and with God.

The meanings of music are necessarily very personal. While words or objects in a painting or the objective reality of a building are symbols which have nearly identical meanings for all who see and use them, the symbols of music are much less precise and permit of widely varying interpretation, depending on the varying experiences of each listener, his receptivity, the particular performance he hears, and even his mood of the moment.

Music is one of the most valuable means available to man for the cultivation of the life of the spirit. Music should be thought of in terms of nourishment, because it speaks to the spirit of man to feed it with a food which is beyond the material. Music gives rise to reflection and contemplation of powers within and without ourselves which cannot be reduced to doctrines or propositions but which are nonetheless real. A great piece of music can sweep away mountains of worry, care, and concern, and free our sight to give us a clearer view of the things that matter. At its best and deepest, music points to God, to His power and mercy, and to the destiny His benevolent grace has prepared for us beyond the music of this time and place.

We said earlier that the significance of music cannot be reduced to an essay on love, for instance, or on any other concrete or philosophical concept. By now we hope that you see with us that the significance of music also cannot be reduced to an essay on music. Talking and writing about music may, if the talk and writing are good, suggest some things to listen for. But we will never apprehend the full significance of music or know all it offers us unless we intently listen to the music itself with the expectation of discovery.

If we listen so, then there will open to us visions of reality and beauty which we can have in no other way. The unique grasp and the unique speech of music insure this reward.

4

Music and Three Persons

To leave our discussion of the powers of music without recognizing their source would leave them, so to speak, dangling in midair, not rooted in anything real or secure. Anyone dealing thoughtfully with music for any length of time realizes that he encounters not disembodied, sourceless powers but a person of whose life the powers are the sign and expression. The reach of music for the ultimate realms and final discoveries is in fact the effort to find and to know God. The quest of music is ultimately a theological activity. It should not surprise us, therefore, to find that in our consideration of that quest Christian theology offers us numerous insights and a matrix for the thoughts of our discussion.

This matrix is the doctrine of the Trinity: one God, but three Persons in the one God. The Bible associates certain activities with each of these Persons, while at the same time recognizing that each Person is indissolubly involved in all the works of God. God the Father is identified as the Creator, Lawgiver, and Preserver. God the Son, who was sent by His Father into the world in the person of Jesus Christ, is the redeemer and the prophet who reveals the truth of God to men. God the Spirit is the sanctifier sent by Jesus Christ to create faith and love in the hearts of men and to give them His power.

For the purposes of our inquiry we shall consider Jesus Christ as the Revealer of Truth and the One who sends the Spirit, the Holy Spirit as the One who gives life and power, and the Father as the Creator and the One who sent Jesus Christ to reveal Himself.

A. THE GOD WHO IS TRUTH

There has been implicit in much that we have already said a conviction that the primary function and value of music is to be found in the realm of truth. We are well aware that this is not a unanimous attitude toward the arts and particularly toward music. People commonly think of music as being primarily concerned with beauty and, even more popularly, with emotion. But we believe, as we have said, that the purpose of music is to discover and reveal meanings. We have identified the discovery of meaning, or truth, as the common obligation of composer, performer, and hearer.

This is certainly the situation in the other arts. We look to painting, literature, and sculpture for a revelation of the reality of things. Even in architecture, which may at first, like music, seem to be far removed from any necessity or power to apprehend and transmit truth, we are impressed finally with the justice or truth of the form and function of great architecture. In the Foreword to the book *Structures,* by Pier Luigi Nervi, the great contemporary Italian engineer and architect, the translator Mario Salvadori says: "If I were asked why Nervi's structures are so keenly admired the world over by architects, engineers, and laymen, my immediate answer would be: 'Because they are so true.'" ([New York: F. W. Dodge Corp., 1956], p. vi)

There is ample evidence for this point of view in music as well. If beauty were the primary goal of music, all that would be necessary would be one lovely sound — just that and nothing more. No development, no exploration, no contending forces, no movement would be needed. Such beauty would be sterile indeed. Furthermore, much great music is not at all beautiful in the sense of pleasant, gratifying, or lovely. Listen to the raw power of Guillaume de Machaut's liturgical music or to the ugly dissonances which Bach employs to denote sin, suffering, and despair. A single-minded search for beauty as a primary goal and at all costs cannot produce such music. Nor can it explain the serious and devoted contemporary composer who has forsworn all easy roads to pleasant beauty and has chosen instead an acid, dissonant style to show us some truths about the human condition.

We cannot know beauty unless we know the truth. This is no mere quibble like the famous debate as to whether the chicken or the egg comes first. To believe that one can know beauty without knowing the truth is to believe that beauty may be found in a vacuum or in a lie. St. Augustine said: "Beauty is the glory of *truth*."

Similarly emotional response is inadequate as the primary goal of music. Emotions require an object. There must be substance or a vision of substance before there can be a reaction. This explains why popular music usually has such a short life. Popular tunes elicit an immediate and sometimes frenzied response. Millions of records are sold. But within a few short months the very people who greeted the tune with such enthusiasm have tired of it, and the tune is heard no more — mercifully, in most cases. There was not enough substance to it. The emotional reaction withered so quickly because it had its roots in soil too shallow. On the other hand, great music which at first may seem austere or even cold somehow fastens on the mind and heart of man and will not let him go. The mature music of Heinrich Schütz and the last works of Beethoven are of this order. They will not sell a million records in the next few months, or perhaps ever, but they have lived vigorous lives for a long time and show unmistakable signs of the ability to continue speaking to succeeding generations.

Certainly the composer, as we have said, wishes his music to speak to the spirit of man and to move him emotionally. But so that his music may do this, he must fasten on an object worthy of deep and abiding response. This is reality — the truth.

Truth in music, of course, is not in the form of words, verbal propositions, or palpable objects or concepts. Nor must truth come only in such forms. Truth can be apprehended intuitively, as when we know that someone loves us. It is in the intuitive grasp and presentation of truth that music makes its contribution.

In the first place, great music, as other great art, has a certain timelessness about it which lifts it and us beyond the temporary and ephemeral. Thus a Claudio Monteverdi madrigal, an Orlando di Lasso motet, a Mozart symphony find echoes in the hearts of men far beyond their own day. There is an inherent verity which transcends the particular and is applicable to persons and situations not at all connected with the time of origin. There is a quality in the music which goes beyond surface beauty and which we can only describe with the words "reality" and "truth."

Secondly, we recognize in great pieces of music a certain order and form which makes them able to communicate clearly and persuasively. Thus a Bach fugue appeals to us as being eternally "right" and "just" because of the inexorable logic which proceeds out of the theme through the variations to the ultimate pedal point and conclusion of the fugue. The music is intelligible intellectually and emotionally because it has been fashioned in a logical and psychologically just and truthful form.

In the third place, there is in all great pieces of art a unity within themselves and with life and other arts which makes them appeal to us as being true. Thus when we hear Dietrich Buxtehude's lovely prelude on "O Sacred Head, Now Wounded," we feel that the composition is right and true within itself as music and at the same time right and true as an expression of Christ's suffering and death. We feel the truth, the appropriateness, of the music even though we do not hear the words at the moment.

At its best and highest, this truth appears in music as a revelation of the unseen — we get a glimpse of the power and glory lying hidden behind the appearances of things. It is a revelation of the eternal and infinite, in a very real sense a vision of the power and the glory of God.

And it is at this point that we remember that it is Christ in whom God revealed *all* truth. The Gospel according to St. John makes this point again and again. "Grace and truth came by Jesus Christ" (John 1:17). Jesus said, "I am the way, the truth, and the life. No man cometh unto the Father but by Me" (John 14:6). On trial for His life before Pilate, Jesus said, "To this end was I born, and for this cause came I into the world, that I should bear witness unto the truth. *Everyone that is of the truth heareth My voice.*" (John 18:37b)

Jesus' claim is that there is no truth apart from Him. Such truth as man derives without knowledge or recognition of the Christ is still dependent on Him and His giving hand. We know nothing apart from Him.

When therefore music grasps and brings us a vision of truth, covered and incomplete though that vision still may be, it is because Christ is seeking to come to man also here. Francis Thompson's poem, "The Hound of Heaven," recounts the flight of man from God and the pursuit of the "Hound of Heaven," who is Christ, for man. Through all of nature, through all thought and experience, the Christ keeps calling to man to acknowledge Him. The call is heard in music also:

> Yet ever and anon a trumpet sounds
> From the hid battlements of Eternity;
> Those shaken mists a space unsettle, then
> Round the half-glimpsèd turrets slowly wash again.

> But not ere him who summoneth
> I first have seen, enwound
> With glooming robes purpureal, cypress-crowned;
> His name I know, and *what his trumpet saith.*

The redeeming and pursuing love of Christ has so arranged all things, including music, that they cannot but speak of Him. Haltingly, it is true, incompletely, and not in the clear terms man finally needs; but clearly enough to tell man that He, the Truth and the Life and the Way, is present, searching for us and anxious to be found.

Musicians may choose to ignore the truth in Christ or to deny it or flee it, as did the man in "The Hound of Heaven." To the extent that their music avoids or denies the truth it will tend toward meaninglessness, obscurity, or falsity. To the extent that they seek the truth and serve it, their music will tend toward meaning, clarity, and truth.

B. THE GOD WHO IS SPIRIT

"Without Me ye can do nothing," said Jesus (John 15:5). Without truth, music is impotent. But music which grasps and speaks truth is powerful, for truth is dynamic. It is of God. Truth generates emotion, activates the will, spurs to activity. Truth, in a word, begets the life of the spirit.

Truth does not have to struggle and strain to accomplish this. It is its nature to capture the being of man and to move him. This explains why a piece of music which has in it the ring of truth also moves us emotionally, quickens and refreshes our spirit, and nourishes us. The revelation of a truth, also in music, can give us a feeling of profound joy. One cannot listen to a great piece of music without feeling its power to move, without knowing that it is animated by a spirit which is more than the total of its sounds, without realizing that its life is beyond any explanation limited to its materials and techniques.

It is here that we must be reminded that Jesus Christ, the Truth, promised that He would send the Spirit. John 15:26 reads: "When the Comforter is come, whom I will send unto you from the Father, even *the Spirit of truth,* which proceedeth from the Father, He shall testify of Me." It should not surprise us that truth begets spirit also in music. If Jesus is the truth and sends the Spirit, we should then expect that music which echoes the truth in Christ, however faintly, will to that extent testify to the power of the Spirit.

Here, as elsewhere in this discussion, we do not equate the finite "truths" and finite "spirits" which man by use of reason and experience of life can deduce with the truth and spirit of God's revelation in Christ. These latter go beyond man's finite capacities to discover. At the same time, we must avoid another extreme, which would see any truth or any resulting spirit as existing apart from the activity of God, who is the Source of all.

The spirit which truthful music engenders is not simply an excitation of emotion. When we considered the power of music to speak, we pointed out that it includes also the power of inciting to action. A little child hearing some delightful music with a persuasive rhythm will typically

64

begin to dance. We all have the experience of wishing to move our bodies in response to the movement of music.

However, the most significant action resulting from music is inner action, which might better be called a change in being. We know from Christian theology that the gifts of the Spirit of God are faith, hope, and love. This is the kind of action which results from the activity of the spirit also in music.

We do not claim that music can bring man to faith in Christ or to hope rooted in Him or to love in the Christian sense. But we do mean to say that just as Christ calls man to acknowledge Him through the truth which can be heard in a piece of music, so much does Christ invite man to come to Him in faith, hope, and love through the spirit which results from that truth. The truth is a desirable, winning, inviting force.

The redeeming and pursuing love of Christ has arranged all things, including music, so that they cannot but invite man to come to Him. The invitation is still veiled and incomplete. But it is clear and attractive enough to hint the Presence behind the mask.

The spirit also tends toward unity. Diversity is a part of life for which we do not need to seek; it is all about us. But unity is much more rare. The perception of the unity which underlies the diversity of things and which is a testimony to the single Creator is a gift of the Spirit which can come only with the truth. Music which has the ring of truth is music in which the discordant, the inharmonious, the perversely dissident, while present as in life, are submerged in the glory of the spirit of truth which dominates and prevails.

To the extent that a musician ignores, denies, or flees the activity of the Spirit of God, to that extent his music will be unstable, empty, negative, or destructive. To the extent that he seeks the Spirit and serves Him, his music will speak of unity, faith, hope, and love.

C. THE GOD WHO IS BEAUTY

Music which speaks truth and which moves our beings in the direction of truth and life is bound to be beautiful. We repeat St. Augustine: *"Beauty* is the glory of truth." Beauty emanates from truth as light from a candle.

And why should not this be so? It is the function of the Son, who is the truth, to show us the Father, who is the creator of all. John 1:18 reads: "No man hath seen God at any time; the only begotten Son, which is in the bosom of the Father, He hath declared Him." It is the function of the Spirit so to warm our hearts that we can come to the Father in faith, as John says: "It is the Spirit that quickeneth" (6:63). And so our eyes are opened to see that "Every good gift and every perfect gift is from above and cometh down from the Father of lights, with whom is no variableness, neither shadow of turning." (James 1:17)

The truth and power of music testify to the Source, the Creator. When He had finished His creation, He looked and "saw every thing that He had made, and, behold, it was very good" (Gen. 1:31). There was a serenity, a glory, an order which mirrored the Creator Himself. The Creator and Source of all beauty had made a beautiful creation.

Note that He had not made creation only that it might be beautiful. Read the first chapter of Genesis again, and see how like a great fugue building to its climax the account of God's creative act steadily develops toward the overwhelming pronouncement that man should subdue and have dominion over every living thing. It is for man, not for beauty, that God has made all that He has made.

Thus beauty is not a purpose but a result. Beauty is the appearance of the works of God. It is a reflection of Him in whom all beauty resides.

The search for beauty as an end in itself, apart from a concern for truth, is an insufficient reason for the creation of art and is doomed to failure. It is sickly. It is a building which strives vainly upward without a firm foundation and which must therefore collapse in rubble. It is a piece of music which screams or wallows, as the case may be, but which cannot attract us with beauty it does not have, because it has rejected what is true.

What then? Is music not to be beautiful? Is the musician to be concerned only with truth and care nothing whether or not his music has beauty? By no means. It is the element of beauty that makes the truth intelligible and provides the spirit its way into the heart of man. It is the search and invitation of God made alluring. It is the proof that we have heard the truth and that the spirit which has moved us is of God. It is an indication that the God who created us approaches us with winning love. Music cannot do without beauty; but beauty cannot exist without truth.

To the extent that music ignores, denies, or flees the Father, in whom all beauty finds its source, it will tend toward disorder and the ugly. To the extent that music seeks the Father and shows Him, it will tend toward order and beauty.

5

Where God and Man Meet

Our train of thought began with an answer to the question, "What is man's purpose in music?" Man's basic purpose is to make and communicate discoveries about the meaning of life. From the standpoint of man, music provides an avenue to truth. We have also seen that God has His purpose for the art of music. It is to find man and call him back to Himself.

The very fact that man conducts a search for God in music and that there God seeks to speak to him is a sign of some estrangement. We are children of God because He has created us, but we have refused our sonship. Now, realizing that something is wrong, we scurry about, looking here and there to find the way back to the Father. But we are in a jungle at midnight. Eventually exhausted, we recognize that the way is lost, apparently forever.

In our dilemma God enters our lives and mercifully calls us back. To the extent that God is permitted to speak in music and we are willing and able to hear Him, music is the voice of redemption. For in music, too, God seeks man in love to call him to reunion. This is a reason why music is beautiful and excites our emotion.

But He does more than call; He comes! There is an

account in the Second Book of Chronicles which illuminates this truth in a marvelous way. Beginning in the second chapter, the story of the building of the temple at Jerusalem is told. For this temple, the symbol of the presence of the Lord and the place where His Word would be spoken, all the riches of the earth were assembled. The symbols of Jehovah's bounty in trees, precious stones, and minerals were joined with the labor of skilled craftsmen to create a testimony of overwhelming splendor to the work and love of God.

Then, on the day of dedication, this is what occurred:

It came even to pass as the trumpeters and singers were as one, to make one sound to be heard in praising and thanking the Lord, and when they lifted up their voice with the trumpets and cymbals and instruments of music and praised the Lord, saying: "For He is good, for His mercy endureth forever," that then the house was filled with a cloud, even the house of the Lord, so that the priests could not stand to minister by reason of the cloud, for the glory of the Lord had filled the house of God. (2 Chron. 5:13, 14)

Here music joins with all else in creation and all else that man can fashion to speak the goodness and mercy of God. But more than that, it is highly significant that it is at the very moment when the music begins that the Lord enters this place and comes to His people.

Notice also the manner of His coming. He is hidden and yet visible. This is how God appears in the symbols of Himself which He has made. An apple tree in summer is not God, but it testifies to His creative hand and to His bounty. The revelation of God in nature is a breakthrough in disguise.

Similarly God seeks to break through the works of men. Also here he is as a cloud — hidden and yet visible. God seeks to use every word, every movement, every sound and color of the artist's product. He seeks to invest with divine significance the common materials, forms, and processes of art. This fact makes it possible for man to fashion symbols of God and references to divine acts.

Since God does seek to meet man in his art, there is no such thing as secular art. All art is either sacred or diabolical. Man speaks for God or for the devil. There is no being neutral.

While therefore God seeks to break through with His message of love and reconciliation, man and the devil can block Him. Man, who can open his eyes, may also close them. God creates, but man and the devil can pervert and destroy. By an act of the Spirit of God, man may become willing to accept the gifts of God, but he is also free to reject both the gift and the Giver.

Such rejection results in an art of negation, emptiness, meaninglessness. Art then becomes arbitrary and quixotic, not rooted in any aspects of reality either within or outside itself. It becomes diabolical art, and in it not God but the devil meets man.

Even when the artist and musician have opened their hearts to the voice and presence of God, they bring to their art certain human weaknesses which muffle the sound and distort the image. Man's weaknesses of perception and will, of creative ability and skill, result in symbols which are

71

inadequate for their task. Inadequate symbols produce inferior music, no matter how pious the composer, no matter how much truth may have been intended, no matter how much truth may be contained in the words to which the music has been set or to which it may refer.

This is precisely what happens in much music written for the church. It is sadly too often the case that while the composers may be excellent Christians, they are unquestionably bad musicians. Too often they ask the God of heaven to talk baby talk. They plead that such bad music is justified because people like it or because it gives people a religious feeling. What a miserable excuse! God's purpose in music is not to please man with agreeable sounds and certainly not to make him feel religious. Church music which starts from such premises is diabolical; in fact, it is all the more of the devil because it distorts and perverts what it pretends to serve.

God and man approach each other in music from opposite directions and with initially differing purposes, but they meet. Man seeks to secure something in music; God seeks to give it. For man, music is search and discovery; for God, it is revelation and redemption. For man, music is both gift and achievement; for God, the Giver, it is only gift.

The Christian Man Responds

And now, how shall we receive the gift? To begin with, do the conclusions we have reached regarding the nature of music and the source of its powers make no difference in our assessment of it? Could we perhaps forget all about God's confrontation and man's discovery?

I think not. For to ignore the activity of one or the other partner is to have an incomplete view of the action which takes place. Man's search becomes futile without God's presence, and God's presence seems pointless without man's search. Christian insights make it possible to see music as it is in reality. And to see music in its reality effects a basic change in the Christian's relation to it.

The Musician

Some things are not changed. The Christian musician, no less than any other, needs to work at his craft. Christian faith supplies no magical inspiration which takes the place of the musician's obligation to learn his craft and to practice it assiduously. The Christian's recognition of the Trinity does not automatically make his music truthful, powerful, or beautiful.

The difference is rather this, that the Christian musician knows the source of the truth, spirit, power, and beauty that he seeks to find in his music and, knowing the source, is better equipped for the search. This knowledge vastly enlarges the area of his concern. He is not earthbound or self-bound. He knows that music limited to the level of sense will result in the same satiety and eventual disgust which reward sensuality in any other area of life. He realizes that music whose appeal is limited to the intellect will leave him and all others cold. He knows that he must search for the whole truth and serve it.

Knowing also that God has granted him and his music such great gifts in order to show His love, the Christian musician can approach his tasks with confident hope that the One who offers will make him able to receive. He can afford to forsake the easy path for the longer, harder, and more rewarding one because he has the promise: "Seek, and ye shall find." (Matt. 7:7)

The Hearer

For most Christians, the question of a proper response to music is not a professional concern. It is rather a question of reacting to music, as to all else in one's environment, with a response which is positively and uniquely Christian. Since God constantly tries to speak to us in our history, in our culture, in all of the events and circumstances of our lives, the Christian man ought constantly to look for divine meaning, for the voice of God, in all that comes before him.

The obligation to make discoveries in music falls upon the Christian with particular force, for he knows more to seek and where it may be found. For him it must be insufficient to find only surface charm, sensuous appeal, or expert craftsmanship. He remains unfulfilled in music if only his emotions are stirred. He must search after the whole truth as God gives the truth.

As he conducts his search for truth in the art of music, he must ask: "Does this ring true?" "Does this music breathe the spirit of life which the truth brings with it?" "Does the beauty of this music point beyond itself?" On the basis of his answers he will identify and reject the demonic and identify and cherish the godly.

There are no easy criteria on which to base these judgments. The quality of truth is not confined to any one historical period or musical style. God is not necessarily present in counterpoint and absent from harmony. Truth may be heard in good jazz, and it may be absent from a motet.

There are also no infallible "authorities" whom one may consult. The centuries-long experience of mankind does indeed provide a clue to the music of reality, for history has a way of discarding the unreal. But mankind is no less fallible than one man.

Finally, however much help one may derive from the experiences of others, the search for truth is a lonely pursuit wherever it is conducted. And this is right, because God calls us one by one.

6

Conclusion

Since the day in Eden when God told man to subdue the earth, man has restlessly explored and experimented. His discoveries appear to be nowhere near the end. As of this writing he is poised to travel to the moon. But all his magnificent achievements in the physical world have failed to provide answers to the most urgent quests of man — those of the spirit.

The arts make a unique contribution to human life in the spiritual quest, for the arts lead through the senses to an awareness beyond sensation. Music is perhaps the most valuable of the arts for culturing such awareness, for its symbols do not have the handicap of literal meaning and therefore are free to speak immediately of spiritual things.

The Christian needs, therefore, to travel also this God-given road to the meaning of the universe. He needs to be wary, because not all the pretty sounds he hears are the voice of God. The Lorelei still sing. Even where the voice of God is heard, God is impatient with our fixation on His voice, and wishes us instead to listen to the burden of His message, which is that He loves us. More than this He has chosen not to say in music. The revelation of God in the person of Jesus Christ is necessary to our redemption and salvation.

But short of this ultimate revelation, music encompasses and speaks to the issues of life to such purpose that we ignore its voice only to our own sad loss.

The function of music is to show us how things are.

This music does through exploration of the mysteries of sound and time.

Certain revelations reward such exploration.

These revelations stand for other mysteries and glories in both the seen and unseen worlds, and even give us an apprehension, as in parable, of the eternal world which we cannot know until God frees our senses in death.

The musician is therefore first of all a prophet — a man called to reveal things past, things present, and things to come. His subjects are God, man, and the universe. His materials are sound and time. His method is explication, making clear, presenting, and explaining.

His reward is the beauty with which God clothes all truth and the knowledge that God works also through him to accomplish His benevolent purposes for man.

The actively Christian listener, knowing that God is there to be heard, must try to discern the voice of God among all the enticing voices appealing for his attention.

For Further Reading

Bacon, Ernst. *Words on Music.* Syracuse: Syracuse University Press, 1960.

Butler, Bartlett R. "Music." Chap. xii in *Christian Faith and the Liberal Arts,* ed. Harold H. Ditmanson, Howard V. Hong, Warren A. Quanbeck. Minneapolis: Augsburg Publishing House, 1960. Pp. 186—202.

Cooke, Deryck. *The Language of Music.* London: Oxford University Press, 1959.

Howes, Frank. *Music and its Meanings.* New York: Oxford University Press, 1958.

Meyer, Leonard B. *Emotion and Meaning in Music.* Chicago: The University of Chicago Press, 1957.

Routley, Erik. *Church Music and Theology.* Philadelphia: Muhlenberg Press, 1959.

Schoenberg, Arnold. *Style and Idea.* New York: Philosophical Library, Inc., 1950.

Sessions, Roger. *The Musical Experience of Composer, Performer, Listener.* Princeton: Princeton University Press, 1950.

Stravinsky, Igor. *Poetics of Music.* Cambridge: Harvard University Press, 1947.

GAYLORD

PRINTED IN U.S.A.